DECORATIVE ART
OF THE
SOUTHWESTERN INDIANS

By
DOROTHY SMITH SIDES

With annotations by
CLARICE MARTIN SMITH

and a Foreword by
FREDERICK WEBB HODGE
Director, Southwest Museum

DOVER PUBLICATIONS, INC.
NEW YORK

Published in Canada by General Publishing Company, Ltd., 30 Lesmill Road, Don Mills, Toronto, Ontario.

Published in the United Kingdom by Constable and Company, Ltd., 10 Orange Street, London WC 2.

This Dover edition, first published in 1961, is an unabridged and corrected republication of the work originally published in portfolio format by the Fine Arts Press, Santa Ana, California, in 1936.

Standard Book Number: 486-20139-2
Library of Congress Catalog Card Number: 62-353

Manufactured in the United States of America
Dover Publications, Inc.
180 Varick Street
New York, N.Y. 10014

FOREWORD

That there was keen appreciation of the art of decoration among the American Indians, and especially on the part of the women, one need only glance at the selection made by the artist-author of this book to be convinced. Indeed so rich in esthetic quality was, and still is, much of the art product of the Indians of the United States alone, that the artist-author has been compelled to confine her immediate attention to that of the Southwest, leaving to the future the extension of her studies, let it be hoped, to the decorative art of the Indians of other fields.

Mrs. Sides has made from a vast amount of material, especially in the Southwest Museum, as comprehensive a selection as possible of the designs on pottery, basketry, and other artifacts of the Southwestern tribes, and in this manner has presented a fair impression of what those Indians have accomplished in early and in later times. The copies were faithfully made, while the reproductions are such as no one can reasonably criticize.

The demand for such a work on primitive art as the present one has grown with the increasing interest in Indian art and beliefs. Schools have undertaken the study of these subjects in a serious way, and there never have been so many devotees of American ethnology as at the present time. We commend the present work as one worthy of an honored place in the growing library of aboriginal American art.

F. W. HODGE

Southwest Museum
Los Angeles, California

ACKNOWLEDGMENTS

Grateful acknowledgment is given to all those who have assisted me. Most especially my Mother, without whose help, both material and mental, there would have been no book. To Florence Daly and Helen Evans, reference librarians of the Riverside Public Library; Winifred W. Britton, former Librarian of the Southwest Museum; Charles Avery Amsden for his timely advice and encouragement, and particularly to Dr. Frederick Webb Hodge, whose kindness, help and well-deserved criticism is most deeply appreciated. Lastly to Thomas E. Williams of the Fine Arts Press, for his courage, perhaps rashness, in printing this book.

LIST OF PLATES

LIST OF PLATES

LIST OF PLATES

LIST OF PLATES

BIBLIOGRAPHY

ALEXANDER, Hartley Burr. Pueblo Indian Painting.
1932 C. Szwedzicki, Nice, France.

AMSDEN, Charles Avery. Black-on-White Ware.
1931 In Kidder, A. V., Pottery of Pecos, vol. I.
Yale University Press, New Haven.

1934 Navaho Weaving.
Fine Arts Press, Santa Ana, California.

BOAS, Franz. The Decorative Art of the Indians of the
1897 North Pacific Coast.
Bulletin of the American Museum of
Natural History, vol. IX, pp. 123-176,
New York.

BUNZEL, Ruth L. The Pueblo Potter.
1930 Columbia University Press, New York.

CHAPMAN, Kenneth M. Evolution of the Bird in Decorative Art.
1916 Art and Archaeology, vol. IV, no. 6, pp.
307-316, Washington.

1931 Indian Pottery.
Exposition of Indian Tribal Arts, New
York.

1933 Pueblo Indian Pottery, vol. I.
C. Szwedzicki, Nice, France.

COOLIDGE, Mary R. The Rain-makers.
1929 Houghton Mifflin Co., Boston and New
York.

CRANE, Leo. Indians of the Enchanted Desert.
1925 Little, Brown & Co., Boston.

1928 Desert Drums.
Little, Brown & Co., Boston.

BIBLIOGRAPHY

CURTIS, Edward S.
1907-1930

The North American Indian, 20 vols.
Cambridge and Norwood, Mass.

DIXON, Joseph K.
1904

The Vanishing Race.
Doubleday, Page & Co., New York.

DOUGLAS, F. H.
1933-1935

Leaflets of the Denver Art Museum, nos.
53-54, 69-70.

FEWKES, Jesse Walter.
1894

Dolls of the Tusayn Indians.
E. J. Brill, Leiden, Holland.

1897

Tusayan Katcinas.
Fifteenth Annual Report Bureau of Ethnology, pp. 245-313, Washington.

1901

Archaeological Expedition to Arizona in 1895.
Seventeenth Annual Report Bureau of American Ethnology, pt. 2, pp. 519-744.

1903

Hopi Katcinas.
Twenty-first Annual Report Bureau of American Ethnology, pp. 3-126, Washington.

1904

Two Summers' Work in Pueblo Ruins.
Twenty-second Annual Report Bureau of American Ethnology, pp. 3-195, Washington.

GODDARD, Pliny Earle.
1903-1904

Life and Culture of the Hupa.
University of California Publication in American Archaeology and Ethnology, vol. I, no. 1, Berkeley.

GUTHE, Carl E.
1925

Pueblo Pottery Making.
Yale University Press, New Haven.

HARRINGTON, Mark R.
1927

Form and Color in American Indian Pottery North of Mexico.
Reprinted from the Journal of American Ceramic Society, vol. X, no. 7, Columbus, Ohio.

HEWETT, Edgar Lee.
1930

Ancient Life in the American Southwest.
Bobbs-Merrill Co., Indianapolis.

BIBLIOGRAPHY

HODGE, Frederick Webb.   Pottery of Hawikuh.
1923   Indian Notes, Museum of the American Indian, Heye Foundation, vol. VII, no. 1, New York.

HOLLISTER, U. S.   The Navaho and his Blanket.
1903   Denver, Colorado.

HOLMES, William H.   Pottery of the Ancient Pueblos.
1886   Fourth Annual Report Bureau of Ethnology, pp. 257-360, Washington.

1888   A Study of the Textile Art in it's Relation to the Development of Form and Ornament.
Sixth Annual Report Bureau of Ethnology, pp. 189-252, Washington.

JAMES, George Wharton.   Indian Basketry.
1901   Privately printed for the author, Pasadena, California.

1914   Indian Blankets and their Makers.
A. C. McClurg & Co., Chicago.

1917   The Indian Secrets of Health.
Radical Life Press, Pasadena, California.

KIDDER, Alfred Vincent.   Pottery of Pecos, vols. I-II.
1931-1936   Yale University Press, New Haven.

KISSELL, Mary L.   Basketry of the Papago and Pima.
1916   Anthropological Papers of the American Museum of Natural History, vol. XVII. pp. 115-264, New York.

KROEBER, A. L.   Types of Indian Culture in California.
1904   University of California Publications in American Archaeology and Ethnology, vol. II, no. 3, pp. 81-103, Berkeley.

Basket Designs of the Indians of North east California.
University of California Publications in American Archaeology and Ethnology, vol. II, no. 4, pp. 105-167, Berkeley.

BIBLIOGRAPHY

LAUT, Agnes C.
1913

Through our Unknown Southwest.
McBride, Nast & Co., New York.

LUMMIS, Charles F.
1893

Spanish Pioneers.
A. C. McClurg & Co., Chicago.

MASON, Otis Tufton.
1894

Woman's Share in Primitive Culture.
D. Appleton & Co., New York.

1904

Aboriginal American Basketry: Studies in a Textile Art without Machinery.
Annual Report of the U. S. National Museum for 1902, pp. 171-548, Washington.

MATTHEWS, Washington.
1883

Navaho Silversmiths.
Second Annual Report Bureau of Ethnology, pp. 167-178.

1884

Navaho Weavers and their Work.
Third Annual Report Bureau of Ethnology, pp. 371-391.

1887

The Mountain Chant.
Fifth Annual Report Bureau of Ethnology, pp. 379-467.

1891

Navaho Dyestuffs.
Annual Report of the Smithsonian Institution, pp. 613-615.

MINDELEFF, Victor.
1891

A Study of Pueblo Architecture; Tusayan and Cibola.
Eighth Annual Report Bureau of Ethnology, pp. 3-228.

NESBIT, Paul H.
1931

The Ancient Mimbreños.
Logan Museum, Beloit College, Wisconsin.

PAYTIAMO, James.
1932

Flaming Arrow's People.
Duffield & Green, New York.

REICHARD, Gladys A.
1928

Social Life of the Navaho Indians.
Columbia University Press, New York.

BIBLIOGRAPHY

ROBERTS, Helen H.
1929

Basketry of the San Carlos Apache.
Anthropological Papers of the American
Museum of Natural History, vol. XXXI,
pt. 3, New York.

ROBINSON, William H.
1928

Under Turquoise Skies.
Macmillan Co., New York.

ROSEBERRY, T. A.
collection of
1915

Illustrated History of Baskets and Plates,
made by California Indians and many
other tribes.
Panama Pacific Exposition.

RUSSELL, Frank.
1908

The Pima Indians.
Twenty-sixth Annual Report Bureau of
American Ethnology, pp. 3-389.

SEYMOUR, Flora W.
1929

The Story of the Red Man.
Longmans, Green & Co., New York.

SLOAN, John.
and
LA FARGE, Oliver.
1931

Introduction to American Indian Art.
Exposition of Indian Arts Inc.,
New York.

SPIER, Leslie.
1933

Yuman Tribes of the Gila River.
University of Chicago Press, Chicago.

STEVENSON, James.
1883

Illustrated Catalogue of the Collections
Obtained from the Indians of New Mexico and Arizona in 1879.
Second Annual Report Bureau of Ethnology, pp. 407-422.

1891

Ceremonial of Hasjelti Dailjis.
Eighth Annual Report of Bureau of Ethnology, pp. 229-285.

STEVENSON, Matilda Coxe.
1904

The Zuñi Indians: their Mythology, Eso-
teric Fraternities, and Ceremonies.
Twenty-third Annual Report Bureau of
American Ethnology, pp. 3-608.

WESTLAKE, Inez B.
1925

American Indian Designs, First Series.
H. C. Perleberg, New York.

BIBLIOGRAPHY

WHITE, Leslie A. The Acoma Indians.
1932 Forty-seventh Annual Report Bureau of American Ethnology, pp. 17-192.

Annual Reports of the Smithsonian Institution for 1884, 1891, 1928.

Annual Reports of the Bureau of American Ethnology for 1880-1881, 1882-1883, 1883-1884, 1884-1885, 1887-1888, 1893-1894, 1896-1897, 1899-1900, 1900-1901, 1901-1902, 1904-1905, 1929-1930.

DECORATIVE ART
OF THE
SOUTHWESTERN INDIANS

Plate 1

PUEBLO VIEJO, ARIZONA. ANCIENT PUEBLO GROUP
POTTERY DESIGNS

Reference:
Two Summers' Work in Pueblo Ruins.
Jesse Walter Fewkes,
Twenty-second Annual Report Bureau of American Ethnology, 1904, pp. 3-195.

a   Plate LXIX, No. 177536a
b   Plate LXVIII, No. 177521
c   Plate LXIX, No. 177558c

The ruins of Pueblo Viejo are in the valley of the Gila river, Graham County, Arizona.

The designs of Pueblo Viejo pottery consist almost entirely of rectangular figures; examples of picture-writing are not found, nor pictures of birds, showing that the ancient inhabitants had not carried decoration beyond the geometrical stage. Their pottery was divided into the following classes; undecorated rough ware, decorated rough ware, undecorated red ware, decorated black-on-white ware, and decorated gray ware. An unusual feature of the decoration is, that the margin of the design is white. The decoration is both on the interior and exterior of vessel, and consists of rectangular bands and series of terraced figures, a prominent characteristic of all ancient pottery from Arizona.

PLATE 1

a

b

c

Plate 2

FOUR MILE RUIN, ARIZONA. ANCIENT PUEBLO GROUP
POTTERY DESIGNS

Reference:
Two Summers' Work in Pueblo Ruins.
Jesse Walter Fewkes,
Twenty-second Annual Report Bureau of American Eth-
nology, 1904, pp. 3-195.

a   Plate XXVI, No. 177203
b   Plate LX, No. 177048a
c   Plate XLI, No. 177223a

Four Mile Ruin is situated about two miles from Taylor, Arizona, and is one of the largest ruins in the vicinity.

The pottery found here, characteristically the same as that from the Chevlon and Homolobi ruins, consists of a decorated, and a rough coiled ware, the former prevailing. There is also a great similarity in the coarse pottery from Four Mile Ruin and that of Pueblo Viejo. The picture-writing on this pottery is highly instructive; bird figures are particularly abundant, also representations of human beings, reptiles, and insects. The picture-writing of each pueblo has an individuality which seems to indicate that it was independently developed, that certain forms or patterns were adapted to special ideals. The cause of this divergence in the designs is no more comprehensible than the difference in the decoration of modern pottery from the various pueblos.

PLATE 2

a

b

c

Plate 3

FOUR MILE RUIN, ARIZONA. ANCIENT PUEBLO GROUP
POTTERY DESIGNS

Reference:
Two Summers' Work in Pueblo Ruins.
Jesse Walter Fewkes,
Twenty-second Annual Report Bureau of American Ethnology, 1904, pp. 3-195.

a   Plate LXIII, No. 177162a
b   Plate XL, No. 177219a
c   Plate LIX, No. 177160b

Figures of birds predominate in the decoration of the pottery from many ancient pueblos. In the delineation of bird figures the artists took strange liberty with nature. In all representations of mythical animals the imagination had full sway. The portrayal was not that of a familiar bird, but a creature of fancy, distorted by mythological conception or the whim of the artist.

Representations of feathers, often highly conventionalized, are freely used in the designs on ancient pottery. One feather symbol is the triangle, a form of which is still present in modern ceremonial paraphernalia. This type of feather design is common, but is more difficult to recognize than that of the ancient Hopi.

PLATE 3

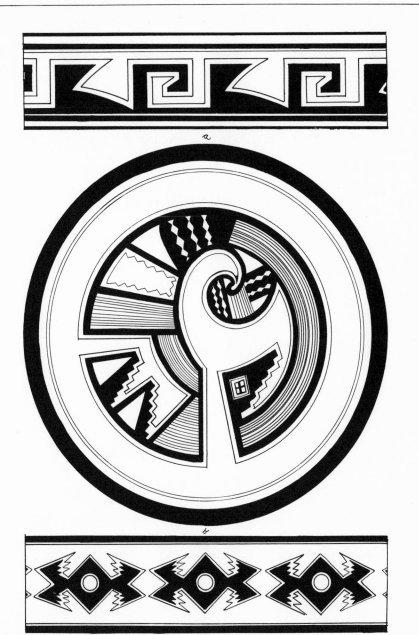

a

b

c

Plate 4

FOUR MILE RUIN, ARIZONA. ANCIENT PUEBLO GROUP
POTTERY DESIGNS

Reference:
Two Summers' Work in Pueblo Ruins.
Jesse Walter Fewkes,
Twenty-second Annual Report Bureau of American Eth-
nology, 1904, pp. 3-195.

a   Page 150, fig. 96, No. 177058
b   Plate XXV, No. 177293a
c   Page 157, fig. 105, No. 157352
d   Plate LXIII, No. 177147b
e   Plate XL, No. 177086b
f   Plate XXV, No. 177110b

The geometric decoration of pottery was common in all ancient pueblos. The
types were terraced figures, spirals, frets, bands, dotes, oblique and zigzag lines. The
proportion of geometric figures to that of animals was large.

The principal decoration was confined to the interior of bowls, but many are
found decorated with external banding. Figures of animals, unless highly conventionalized, and spirial designs, are rare, although straight lines and rectangular figures
were often employed.

Symbolic rain-cloud forms, combining the rectangle, semicircle, and the triangle, were freely used, the rectangle being the most common.

PLATE 4

a   b   c   d   e   f

Plate 5

MIMBRES, NEW MEXICO. ANCIENT PUEBLO GROUP
POTTERY DESIGNS

References:
Southwest Museum
The Ancient Mimbreños
Paul H. Nesbit
Ancient Life in the American Southwest
Edgar Lee Hewett

a
b
c   Specimens from Southwest Museum
d
e

Ruins in the valley of the Rio Mimbres extend from an unknown distance below Deming to the headwaters of the stream in southeastern New Mexico.

The pottery is black-on-white ware and the standard form is the bowl, which is relatively deep and well finished. The decoration is usually confined to the interior of the bowl; the design is well executed, with a delicacy of line and an accuracy of spacing unequaled in other ancient pottery of the Southwest.

Aside from the extraordinary geometric designs, there is a profusion of naturalistic drawings, ranging from evidently mythical figures, to birds, animals, fishes, insects, and human beings.

True naturalism is so rare a phenomenon in all Southwestern pottery decoration, particularly in its early phases, marked by black-on-white wares, that its very high development is puzzling.

Certain bowls used as mortuary vessels, being placed over the head in burials, were always pierced in the base or "killed" to allow the egress of the spirit of the vessel to accompany the soul of the dead to its future world.

PLATE 5

Plate 6

MIMBRES, NEW MEXICO. ANCIENT PUEBLO GROUP POTTERY DESIGNS

References:
The Ancient Mimbreños
Paul H. Nesbit
Ancient Life in the American Southwest
Edgar Lee Hewett
Indian Pottery
Kenneth M. Chapman

a Page 352, Edgar Lee Hewett
b Page 352, Edgar Lee Hewett
c Page 352, Edgar Lee Hewett
d Page 352, Edgar Lee Hewett
e Page   9, Kenneth M. Chapman
f Page 352, Edgar Lee Hewett

The ancient Mimbres people probably surpassed all other ancient Pueblo groups in their art, but they continued to live in pit houses, owing to the intense heat of the Mimbres valley. Although their living conditions remained the same, it was not so with their pottery.

All forms of corrugated ware, used principally for cooking, were familiar to them, and consisted mostly of food bowls with a gray background and black decoration; occasionally there is found black-on-white ware. Their geometric designs were not superior to those of potters of the western slope; however, their life forms were most striking, and in these motifs they were master artists.

These potters developed an esthetic imagination which produced an abundance of beautiful earthenware. The Mimbres valley is rightfully termed an "Ancient Art Province."

PLATE 6

a

b

c

d

e

f

Plate 7

Reference:

Archeological Expedition to Arizona in 1895.
Jesse Walter Fewkes,
Seventeenth Annual Report Bureau of American Ethnology, 1901, pt. 2, pp. 519-744.

a   Plate CXXXII, e
b   Plate CXXXIV, a
c   Plate CXXXII, c
d   Plate CXXIII, c
e   Plate CXXIV, b
f   Plate CXXXV, b

The commonly accepted definition of Sikyatki, "yellow house," so far as the general color of the pueblo is concerned, does not seem to be particularly appropriate; but the name may refer to a cardinal point, a method of symbolic nomenclature followed in the Southwest. The origin of Sikyatki is doubtful, however its builders and occupants are supposed to have come into Hopiland from the valley of the Rio Grande in late prehistoric times. It is almost impossible to estimate the population of this pueblo at the time it flourished, but probably it did not exceed three hundred to five hundred.

PLATE 7

Plate 8

SIKYATKI, ARIZONA. ANCIENT PUEBLO GROUP
HOPI PROVINCE
POTTERY DESIGNS

Reference:
Archeological Expedition to Arizona in 1895.
Jesse Walter Fewkes,
Seventeenth Annual Report Bureau of American Ethnology, 1901, pt. 2, pp. 519-744.

a   Plate CLII, d
b   Plate CLVII, a
c   Plate CLIII, b
d   Plate CXLVIII, d
e   Plate CXLVII, d
f   Plate CXLVII, e
g   Plate CL, a
h   Plate CXLVIII, c
i   Plate CLIV, b
j   Plate CLI, c

Sikyatki pottery is divided into three classes: (1) coiled and indented ware; (2) smooth, undecorated ware; (3) polished decorated ware. This pottery shows little or no duplication in decorative design, and every object bears different symbols. The decoration is chiefly on the interior of bowls, with geometric designs on the upper exterior. The first class, coiled ware, is coarse, not polished, and usually not decorated; the second class, undecorated ware, is as fine as that with painted designs; the third class, polished ware, of which there is the greatest amount, has more or less complicated designs and for this reason affords a more alluring subject for study than the other two classes.

PLATE 8

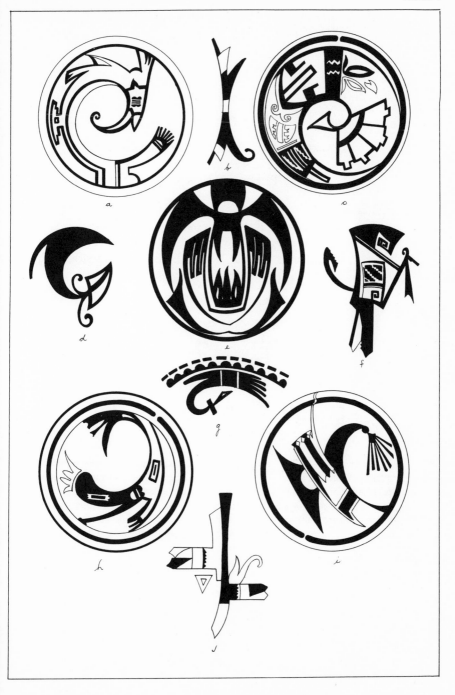

Plate 9

SIKYATKI, ARIZONA. ANCIENT PUEBLO GROUP
HOPI PROVINCE
POTTERY DESIGNS

Reference:
Archeological Expedition to Arizona in 1895.
Jesse Walter Fewkes,
Seventeenth Annual Report Bureau of American Ethnology, 1901, pt. 2, pp. 519-744.

a   Page 708, fig. 286
b   Page 709, fig. 289
c   Page 709, fig. 290
d   Page 709, fig. 292
e   Page 713, fig. 306
f   Page 721, fig. 329
g   Page 723, fig. 337
h   Page 726, fig. 347

In the decoration of Sikaytki ware mythical concepts are sometimes portrayed, as the plumed snake. Reptiles, frogs, tadpoles, and insects are also fairly common. Plants and leaves are seldom employed, but flowers are sometimes used. Probably the most general motif found on the decorated pottery of Sikyatki is the feather, conventionalized, an important feature in the decoration of ancient Sikyatki and other Southwestern pottery. The employment of naturalistic ornament led to the use of rich and varied colors, chiefly yellow, red, black, and white.

PLATE 9

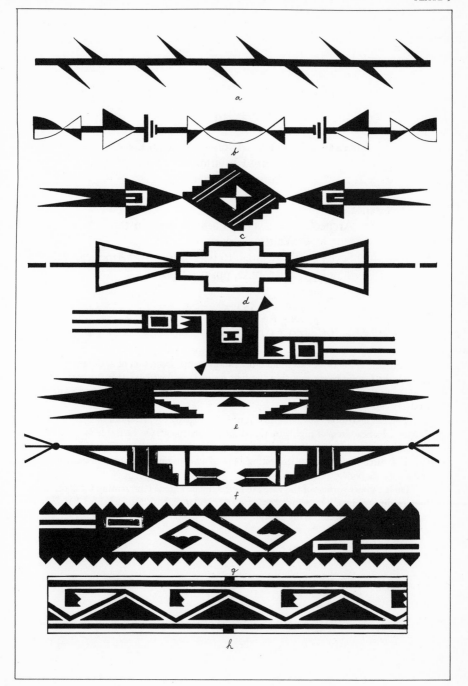

Plate 10

Reference:
Archeological Expedition to Arizona in 1895.
Jesse Walter Fewkes,
Seventeenth Annual Report Bureau of American Ethnology, 1901, pt. 2, pp. 519-744.

a   Page 722, fig. 335
b   Page 683, fig. 272, plate CXXXVII, a
c   Plate CXLIV, a

Birds and feathers far exceed all other motifs in the decoration of ancient Sikyatki pottery, the former being probably the first animal employed for that purpose. The food bowls thus decorated supply an abundance of material for scientific and esthetic study.

There is no reasonable doubt that figure 272, page 683, represents a bird, to which is attached a headdress of highly modified feather ornament. On each side of the body are undoubtedly wings, with feathers continued into arrowpoints. The tail is composed of three large feathers projecting beyond two triangular extensions, marking the end of the body.

On the upper surface of the vase are four similar designs representing birds of the four cardinal points. The wings consist of triangular extensions; each bird has four tail-feathers and rain-clouds on the anterior end of the body.

PLATE 10

a

b

c

Plate 11

Reference:
Two Summers' Work in Pueblo Ruins.
Jesse Walter Fewkes,
Twenty-second Annual Report Bureau of American Ethnology, 1904, pp. 3-195.

a   Page 117, fig. 73, No. 157771
b   Page 114, fig. 69, No. 157769
c   Page 114, fig. 68, No. 157817
d   Plate LI, No. 157784 a
e   Plate L, b
f   Page 117, fig. 72, No. 157134
g   Page 115, fig. 70, No. 157714

Comparatively little pottery has been excavated at the ancient site of the Hopi pueblo of Shongopovi, but the majority of that found consists of fine yellow ware smoothly polished and elaborately decorated. There is no essential difference in the forms of the pottery from this ruin and that from the pueblos on the Little Colorado. The picture-writing on Shongopovi ware closely resembles that on ware from ruins near the East Mesa of Hopiland. On the whole, old Shongopovi pictography is very similar to that of Sikyatki. Specimen b is an entirely different representation of the plumed snake, the feathers being represnted by two semicircular figures and the tongue by a line terminating in an arrowpoint. Many bird forms are present, with a close likeness to those of Sikyatki. A peculiar conventionalized form of "breath feather" here may lead one to regard this as a part of the mythical bird-man god.

PLATE 11

a

b

c

d

e

f

g

Plate 12

HOMOLOBI, ARIZONA. ANCIENT PUEBLO GROUP
POTTERY DESIGNS

Reference:

Two Summers' Work in Pueblo Ruins
Jesse Walter Fewkes,
Twenty-second Annual Report Bureau of American Ethnology, 1904, pp. 3-195.

a Plate XXII, No. 157588, a
b Page 82, fig. 37, No. 156888
c Plate XLIII, No. 156494, b
d Page 76, fig. 31, No. 156603
e Plate XXXIII, No. 156489, b
f Plate XXXII, No. 156621, b

While four ruins are called Homolobi, ruin no. 1, situated three miles from Winslow, Arizona, is designated as the true Homolobi. It was a small pueblo of irregular shape, one exceptional feature of which is that the pottery was not buried with the dead as customary mortuary offerings.

Many beautiful examples of pottery have been found not far from the ruins of Homolobi, covered with pictographs which closely resemble those found in other parts of the pueblo area.

PLATE 12

a

b

c

d

e

f

Plate 13

References:

Pueblo Indian Pottery, vol. 1, 1933.
Kenneth M. Chapman
Leaflets of the Denver Art Museum, 1933-1935,
Nos. 53-54, 69-700.
F. H. Douglas

a No. 61, Leaflets of the Denver Art Museum
b Plate 28, Chapman
c No. 6, Plate 31, Chapman

The pottery of the present pueblo of Tesuque, New Mexico, was until recently quite distinctive from that of the other pueblos, the warm grayish slip being decorated in black only. The designs were complex, being built up of familiar symbols—the trefoil, meander, naturalistic leaf forms, and the plumed serpent which was typical of all Pueblo designs. These in combination form unique decorative elements.

Tesuque potters of the present generation have unfortunately given up the production of this traditional ware and now either imitate the products of other Pueblos or produce quantities of small earthenware articles gaudily decorated with aniline colors and designed solely for sale to white tourists.

PLATE 13

a

b

c

Plate 14

PECOS, NEW MEXICO. PUEBLO GROUP
POTTERY DESIGNS

References:
Pottery of Pecos, vols. I-II, 1931-1936.
Alfred Vincent Kidder
Black-on-White Ware
Charles Avery Amsden
In A. V. Kidder, Pottery of Pecos, vol. I, 1931.

a   Page 69, fig. 18, a
b   Page 79, fig. 24, f
c   Page 69, fig. 18, b
d   Page 65, fig. 16, d
e   Page 149, fig. 90, k
f   Page 115, fig. 68, b
g   Page 69, fig. 18, d
h   Page 87, fig. 34, h
i   Page 69, fig. 18, h

The pueblo of Pecos, abandoned in 1838, was known to have been inhabited as early as 1200 A. D. The pueblo became one of the largest and most important in the Southwest.

The Pecos women were excellent potters, and as their mode of living required pottery for cooking and serving food, as well as for carrying and storing water, a variety of receptacles were manufactured.

A profusion of black-on-white ware will be found, also a biscuit type consisting of a light tan or brown background with a black design. The interior of the bowls was the favorite area for the Pecos decorator; the design was usually in bands which began a little below the rim and extended to the line forming the bottom. Gradually the style changed and many new designs were introduced.

PLATE 14

Plate 15

CHEVLON, ARIZONA. ANCIENT PUEBLO GROUP
(SHAKWABAIYKI)
POTTERY DESIGNS

Reference:
Two Summers' Work in Pueblo Ruins
Jesse Walter Fewkes,
Twenty-second Annual Report Bureau of American Ethnology, 1904, pp. 3-195.

a   Plate XXXVIII, a No. 157119
b   Page 78, fig. 33, No. 157264
c   Page 83, fig. 38, No. 156138
d   Page 79, fig. 34, No. 157084
e   Plate XXXV, a No. 157406
f   Plate XXXVIII b No. 157184

The Chevlon ruin called Shakwabaiyki by the Hopi, or Blue Running Water Pueblo, is near Winslow, Arizona. The country at this point is sandy and almost barren of vegetation.

The pottery from Chevlon is distinctive, and excellent in craftmanship, with a general likeness to that from other Arizona localities. It is more varied in character than that from the true Hopi ruins, though in decoration there is much resemblance. While in the ruins of Chevlon there were many glazed bowls, pots, and jars, at Sikyatki no glazed pottery was found.

PLATE 15

a

b

c

d

e

f

Plate 16

Development of Bird Symbols
Pottery Designs

Reference:

Evolution of the Bird in Decorative Art.
Kenneth M. Chapman,
Art and Archaeology, vol. IV, No. 6, 1916, pp. 307-316.

Of all forms employed as decorative motifs in primitive art, the bird has had the most widespread use. It has been a most adequate symbol in all aboriginal American art and particularly in the Pueblo area. The restricted use of conventionalized life forms is felt in the decoration of pottery, in which many motifs are taken from textile or basketry designs and retain their angular character though continually repeated.

Two types of pottery have furnished a profusion of material for the study of bird motifs, the biscuit ware and glazed ware from Pajarito Plateau of New Mexico. The greatest variety of treatment is found in the symbols from the glazed ware, and a large collection of these figures shows an unusual change from the realistic to forms which bear no resemblance to birds.

PLATE 16

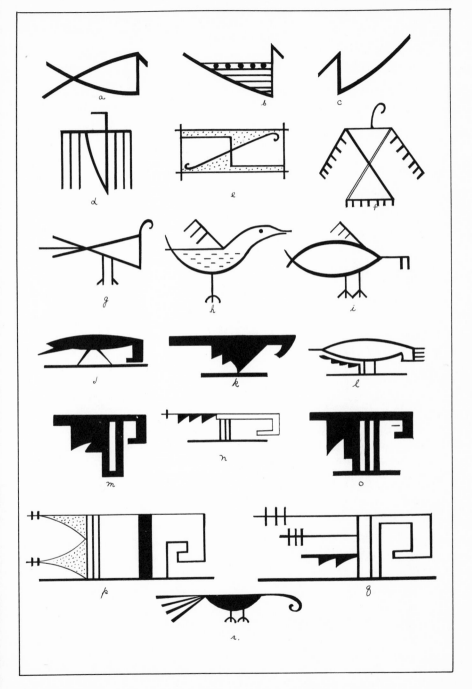

Plate 17

TRIBAL BIRD FORMS
POTTERY DESIGNS

Reference:

Evolution of the Bird in Decorative Art.
Kenneth M. Chapman,
Art and Archaeology, vol. IV, No. 6, 1916, pp. 307-316.

a Page 316, San Ildefonso
b Page 316, San Ildefonso
c Page 316, Zuñi
d Page 315, Zuñi
e Page 315, Zuñi
f Page 316, Acoma
g Page 316, Acoma
h Page 316, Hopi
i Page 316, Hopi

In bird designs the rectangular form of a crooked head is the dominant characteristic. The greatest divergence is found in that part of each figure corresponding with the tail in the more realistic bird; this comes under the division of serrate, stepped, triangular, or linear, and is sometimes double or multiple in form.

The production of pottery is still an important industry in most of the Pueblos of New Mexico and Arizona. The designs of Cochiti and Santo Domingo, neighboring pueblos, show great similarity, though even here some small distinction is easily discovered.

PLATE 17

Plate 18

HOPI KACHINAS

References:
Hopi Katcinas.
Jesse Walter Fewkes,
Twenty-first Annual Report Bureau of American Ethnology, 1903, pp. 13-126.
Tusayan Katcinas,
Jesse Walter Fewkes,
Fifteenth Annual Report Bureau of Ethnology, 1897, pp. 39-48.
Dolls of the Tusayan Indians
Jesse Walter Fewkes

a Sio Humis Kachina, Southwest Museum
b Plate XXXIII, Hokyana Kachina, 21st Report
c Plate XXXIX, Kau Kachina, 21st Report
d Sio Kachina, Southwest Museum

The Hopi Indians represent their gods in several ways, one of which is by personations, which are supposed to have magic power, capable of action for good or evil.

Various symbols have been adopted to represent this power, and are portrayed by "Kachinas" which are objects carved from wood or modeled in clay. The greatest care is given to the representation of the head, and its size is generally out of proportion to the other parts. It is painted in gay colors with various symbols.

Each clan, it seems, as it joined the Hopi population, brought its own gods represented by their kachinas. These were given to their children who were taught the tribal legends, the heroic deeds of their ancestors, and the virtues of truth, honesty, and chastity, by the medicine-men or the old women. Each doll has a name and different characteristic markings; the representation of clouds, in some form, is very general, and is supposed to have a spiritual significance, regarding water as the symbol of the spirit, and prayer for rain—a prayer for that spiritual strength which comes only through opening the heart to God.

PLATE 18

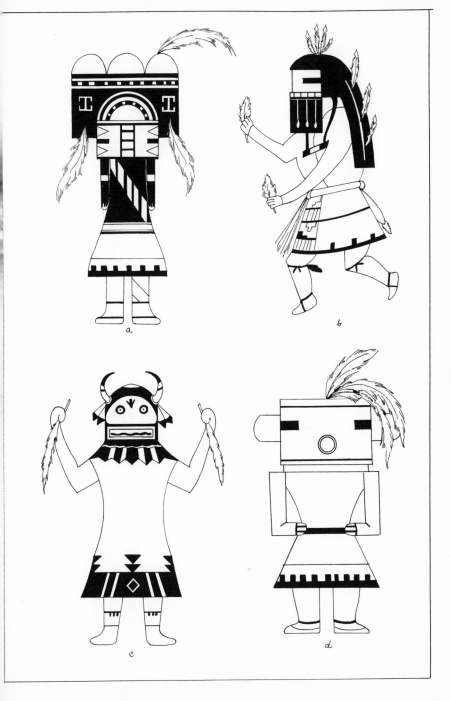

Plate 19

SIA, NEW MEXICO. PUEBLO GROUP
POTTERY DESIGNS

References:
Leaflets of the Denver Art Museum, 1933-1935,
Nos. 53-54, 69-70.
F. H. Douglas
Pueblo Pottery Making
Carl E. Guthe
Southwest Museum

a   No. 64, F. H. Douglas
b   No. 66, F. H. Douglas
c   Plate III c, Carl E. Guthe
d   Southwest Museum

Velino Shigi is an example of an Indian artist who has become very well known; he finished the fifth grade in the Government school at Santa Fe, when, untaught in the art of drawing or color, he was allowed to go on in the native method, in which no one can teach the Indian, and as a consequence one finds many beautiful examples of his art. With the Indian there is never any experiment with color or design, as the picture is mentally completed and then executed with precision.

PLATE 19

a

b

c

d

Plate 20

SIA, NEW MEXICO. PUEBLO GROUP
POTTERY DESIGNS

References:
Southwest Museum.
Dorothy Smith Sides, collection of.

a Flower motif, Dorothy Smith Sides
b Circular design, Dorothy Smith Sides
c Flower motif, Dorothy Smith Sides
d Circular design, Southwest Museum

The pueblo of Sia is on the Jemez river, 16 miles from Bernalillo, New Mexico. Originally its population was very large; it has decreased, however, until at the present it is one of the poorest, with only 150 inhabitants. The Sia women make an excellent pottery which closely resembles the representative type of Acoma. The colors used are red and black on a cream slip and is very often decorated with plant and animal forms, especially birds.

The particular combination and arrangement which is found at Acoma occurs again and again at Sia. In fact, so similar are they that often it would be impossible to tell from the decoration alone whether a jar came from Acoma or Sia. However, the clay of Sia is coarse and heavy, while that of Acoma is extraordinarily light and fine.

PLATE 20

a

b

c

d

Plate 21

SAN ILDEFONSO, NEW MEXICO. PUEBLO GROUP
ANCIENT POLYCHROME PATTERNS

References:
Southwest Museum
Pueblo Pottery Making
    Carl E. Guthe
The Rain-makers
    Mary R. Coolidge
The Pueblo Potter
    Ruth Bunzel
Pueblo Indian Painting
    Hartley Burr Alexander
Pueblo Indian Pottery, vol. 1, 1933
    Kenneth M. Chapman

a   Plate 25, No. 7, Chapman
b   Plate 25, No. 14, Chapman
c   Plate 35,   Guthe
d   Plate 4, No. b, Guthe

San Ildefonso, an exceptionally interesting village of only about 100 inhabitants, is situated on the Rio Grande, not far from Santa Fe. The earthenware is of fine quality and exquisitely modeled, the beauty of a vessel depending upon the perfection of finish; ornament is merely to show by contrast the loveliness of the deep lustrous polish. The colors used in decorating the pottery are minerals, mostly ochres, with the exception of black, which comes from the guaco or Rocky Mountain bee plant.

With these people pottery is an important and profitable industry which has grown so steadily that its production has brought prosperity to the pueblo.

PLATE 21

Plate 22

SAN ILDEFONSO, NEW MEXICO. PUEBLO GROUP
MODERN POLYCHROME, BLACK ON BLACK, RED ON RED WARE

References:
Southwest Museum
Pueblo Pottery Making
Carl E. Guthe
The Rain-makers
Mary R. Coolidge
The Pueblo Potter
Ruth Bunzel
Pueblo Indian Painting
Hartley Burr Alexander
Pueblo Indian Pottery, vol. 1, 1933
Kenneth M. Chapman
Introduction to American Indian Art, 1931
John Sloan and Oliver La Farge

a   Southwest Museum
b   Southwest Museum
c   Southwest Museum
d   Plate XVII, John Stone and Oliver La Farge

The outstanding feature of San Ildefonso design is its restraint and brevity of expression; line is very important, and, too, the potters expend infinite time and pains in the process of polishing. They have developed a great variety of forms and decorations; their ware consits of a polished red, black-and-red on a light slip, and a polished black with designs in dull black. On all bowls the decoration is executed within bands which show considerable variety based on a small number of motifs. The most frequent decoration is the repetition of a single unit. The perfection of each piece depends on the precision of the maker.

PLATE 22

a

b

c

d

Plate 23

References:
> Southwest Museum
> Pueblo Pottery Making
> Carl E. Guthe
> The Rain-makers
> Mary R. Coolidge
> The Pueblo Potter
> Ruth Bunzel
> Collection of Mrs. Kenneth Worthen
> Pueblo Indian Pottery, vol. 1, 1933
> Kenneth M. Chapman

a Mrs. Kenneth Worthen, collection of
b Mrs. Kenneth Worthen, collection of
c Page 125, No. 17, appendix 3, plate XXXVI, Ruth Bunzel
d Page 125, No. 23, appendix 3, plate XXXVI, Ruth Bunzel
e Page 126, No. 28, appendix 3, plate XXXVIII, Ruth Bunzel

Although polished black ware has been typical of San Ildefonso pottery since early times, it was not until Maria Martínez and her husband Julian, discovered, in 1921, the method of applying designs in self color, that this type of modern ceramics came into existence. She fashions her jars and bowls with such art that she has lifted her product into a class by itself. Her pieces are always graceful in form, admirable in design, thin and well fired, and altogether stamped with a brilliance of artistry that commands one's highest admiration. The painting is done usually by Julian.

PLATE 23

Plate 24

References:
Illustrated Catalogue of the Collections Obtained from the Indians of New Mexico and Arizona in 1879.
James Stevenson,
Second Annual Report Bureau of Ethnology, 1883, pp. 307-465.
Introduction to American Indian Art
John Sloan and Oliver La Farge

a   Fig. 618, No. 39581, James Stevenson
b   Plate XVI, Ancient Acoma, John Sloan and Oliver LaFarge
c   Fig. 619, No. 41316, James Stevenson

In western central New Mexico is the Pueblo of Acoma, "The City of the Sky," built 7000 feet above sea-level on a rocky mesa seventy acres in area with perpendicular walls fifty-seven feet high. The pueblo is reached by precipitous clefts, up which all material was carried to build the village. It is inhabited to-day and may be reached by these same paths

Acoma was first visited by Spaniards in the year 1540. The story of the wars fought on this mighty rock is so thrilling as to hold one spellbound.

Of all Indians, none are more resentful of intrusion than the people of Acoma, who are unwilling to impart any real knowledge of themselves.

PLATE 24

Plate 25

ACOMA, NEW MEXICO. PUEBLO GROUP
POTTERY DESIGNS

References:
Illustrated Catalogue of the Collection Obtained from
the Indians of New Mexico and Arizona in 1879.
James Stevenson,
Second Annual Report Bureau of Ethnology, 1883, pp.
307-465.
Southwest Museum

a   Fig. 621, No. 41318, James Stevenson
b   Southwest Museum
c   Fig. 622, No. 42377, James Stevenson

In the pottery of Acoma one will find designs of trees, leaves, birds, and flowers, combined with geometric patterns; the colors used are black, red, and a creamy gray. The ware of Acoma is highly prized for its thinness and lightness, as well as for the wide range of its charming decoration.

The first delicate hair line around the top of a jar is never quite closed, the opening or space thus left is the "exit trail of life" through which the soul of the vessel may make its exit, for to the Indians every object is animate.

In addition to jars made for domestic use, there are vessels set aside for ceremonials. Sometimes funerary vessels were made solely for depositing with the dead.

PLATE 25

a

b

c

Plate 26

References:
Southwest Museum
Pueblo Indian Pottery, vol. 1, 1933.
Kenneth M. Chapman

a   Southwest Museum
b   Southwest Museum
c   Southwest Museum

The pueblo of Santo Domingo is on the east bank of the Rio Grande in north central New Mexico. It is the most conservative of the pueblos, and the people are very jealous of white interference in their affairs. Pottery is still made by the women, who form a heavy white ware with bold designs in black. The use of religious symbols for decoration is forbidden, and the breaking of this rule would be severely punished. Their vessels include large and small bowls, ollas, and huge storage jars, which serve occasionally as drums.

PLATE 26

a

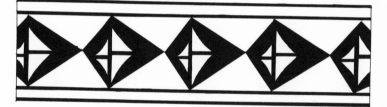

b

c

Plate 27

SANTO DOMINGO, NEW MEXICO. PUEBLO GROUP
POTTERY DESIGNS

References:
Southwest Museum
Pueblo Indian Pottery, vol. 1, 1933.
Kenneth M. Chapman

a   Southwest Museum
b   Southwest Museum
c   Southwest Museum
d   Southwest Museum

Santa Domingo slip, when applied, does not need to be polished with a stone, as is necessary with much of the Pueblo pottery.

The decorative art of Santo Domingo had been held to a severely geometrical system until the beginning of the present century, when the use of red, and the elaboration of plant motifs, led to the notable enrichment of the ancient art. The sacred combination of cloud, lightning, and rain symbols is still tabu, and these, if used singly, are hidden in formal arrangements of geometric and other units.

The "path of the spirit" or "exit trail of life" is often bounded by parallel lines extending vertically from rim to base.

PLATE 27

a

b

c

d

Plate 28

References:
Illustrated Catalogue of the Collection Obtained from
the Indians of New Mexico and Arizona in 1879.
James Stevenson,
Second Annual Report Bureau of Ethnology, 1883, pp.
307-465.

a   Fig. 367, No. 40317
b   Fig. 362, No. 41150
c   Fig. 363, No. 41158
d   Fig. 360, No. 39916

The Zuñi, who once occupied six pueblos, which through misunderstanding
were called the "Seven Cities of Cibola," now live in a single permanent village and
three summer pueblos on the Zuñi River in western New Mexico. They are a highly
developed people, both physically and mentally. From early times they were not only
skilled architects, but accomplished potters, weavers, and farmers, raising their crops
both by dry-farming and by irrigation.

Their ceremonies, elaborate and numerous, are often performed by masked personages who wear highly colored costumes replete with symbolism.

PLATE 28

a

b

c

d

Plate 29

Zuñi, New Mexico. Pueblo Group
Pottery Designs

References:
Illustrated Catalogue of the Collection Obtained from
the Indians of New Mexico and Arizona in 1879.
James Stevenson,
Second Annual Report Bureau of Ethnology, 1883, pp.
307-465.

a   Fig. 427, No. 40290
b   Fig. 361, No. 39934, bird form
c   Fig. 428, No. 39954, leaf and butterfly ornament
d   Fig. 363, No. 41158, bird form
e   Fig. 361, No. 39934, Helix freely used
f   Fig. 363, No. 41158

Zuñi designs are conspicuous for their simplicity, balance, rhythm, abstraction, surpassing range of elements, and virility. These designs, which are of a type that has a recognized value of its own; consist chiefly of triangular figures, open circles, diamonds, scrolls, and arches. The pottery designs are usually divided into zones, and there is a rare combination of patterns; one never finds a meander or Greek fret, and there is a complete absence of vines and floral devices, except that on many of the water jars appear a conventionalized sunflower.

The colors employed in Zuñi pottery ornamentation are cream for the background, with black, red, and brown for the patterns.

PLATE 29

a

b

c

d

e

f

Plate 30

Zuñi, New Mexico. Pueblo Group
Pottery Designs

References:

Illustrated Catalogue of the Collection Obtained from the Indians of New Mexico and Arizona in 1879.
James Stevenson,
Second Annual Report Bureau of Ethnology, 1883, pp. 307-465.

a   Fig. 361, No. 39934, decoration belongs to third variety of design.
b   Fig. 401, No. 40486, outside bowl design
c   Fig. 362, No. 41150, bird form
d   Fig. 360, No. 39916, Helix
e   Fig. 365, No. 40312, bird form
f   Fig. 365, No. 40312
g   Fig. 362, No. 41150

Notwithstanding the oppression of the Spaniards in early times, the culture and esthetic ability of the Zuñis flourished unabated, and they are still producing excellent examples of their craft.

The colors of the Zuñis have a distinct significance. North is designated as yellow, because the light of morning and evening in winter is yellow; West is blue, for westward is the Pacific Ocean; South is red, it being the region of summer, and the East is designated as white, to signify dawn. The upper region is multicolored, as the light of the sun on clouds; the nether region, black, as deep caverns and springs.

PLATE 30

Plate 31

Laguna, New Mexico. Pueblo Group
Pottery Designs

References:

Illustrated Catalogue of the Collection Obtained from the Indians of New Mexico and Arizona in 1879.
James Stevenson,
Second Annual Report Bureau of Ethnology, 1883, pp. 307-465.

a   Fig. 585, No. 41295, broad oblique stripes and a figure resembling blades of corn.

b   Fig. 616, No. 41297, little similarity to any other decoration it contains a scroll and abstract figures.

c   Fig. 588, No. 42386, large flower ornaments surrounding birds with a crest, and serrated figures. One bird represents a raven, the other a California quail.

d   Fig. 587, No. 42381, leaves designed to represent corn blades, partially symbolical.

Laguna, the largest of all the Pueblo settlements east of the Continental Divide, is situated on the south bank of the San José river, forty-five miles west of Albuquerque, New Mexico. It is made up of a central pueblo, with a number of smaller ones. The Lagunas are of exceptional intellect and physical development.

The Laguna dwellings are chiefly two-story adobe structures, architecturally superior in point of construction to those of many Pueblos.

PLATE 31

a

b

c

d

Plate 32

LAGUNA, NEW MEXICO. PUEBLO GROUP
POTTERY DESIGNS

References:
Illustrated Catalogue of the Collection Obtained from
the Indians of New Mexico and Arizona in 1879.
James Stevenson,
Second Annual Report Bureau of Ethnology, 1883, pp.
307-465.

a   Fig. 613, No. 42473, symbolical leaf design.
b   Fig. 615, No. 42471, circular and leaf designs.
c   Fig. 610, No. 42380, oblique bars extending from a
center diamond.
d   Fig. 586, No. 42385, undulating bands and triangles
in alternate enclosed and upper space.
e   Fig. 592, No. 41298, well formed design with no interest.

The Laguna men are engaged in agriculture and stock raising, while the women,
in common with all other Pueblo tribes, are the potters. They produce a variety of
exquisite vessels with designs of flowers and bird forms in red and black on a white
ground. The pottery is beautifully made, exceptionally well designed, and sym-
metrically executed.

PLATE 32

a

b

c

d

e

Plate 33

COCHITI, NEW MEXICO. PUEBLO GROUP
POTTERY DESIGNS

References:
Illustrated Catalogue of the Collection Obtained from
the Indians of New Mexico and Arizona in 1879.
James Stevenson,
Second Annual Report Bureau of Ethnology, 1883, pp.
307-465.
Introduction to American Indian Arts, 1931,
John Sloan and Oliver La Farge
The Rain-makers
Mary R. Coolidge

a   Fig. 39733, No. 623, James Stevenson.
b   Southwest Museum
c   Fig. 39717, No. 631, James Stevenson.
d   Fig. 39726, No. 638, James Stevenson.
e   Fig. 39718, No. 633, James Stevenson.
f   John Sloan and Oliver La Farge.
g   Fig. 39733, No. 623, James Stevenson.
h   Fig. 39562, No. 640, James Stevenson.
i   Fig. 39726, No. 638, James Stevenson.

Cochiti is on the west side of the Rio Grande, twenty-five miles southwest of Santa Fe. Although now of small population, the people of this pueblo claim the ruined towns to the north of their village as the homes of their ancestors. While sharing in the revival of the Pueblo arts and crafts, the ancient symbolism and ceremonies of Cochiti are well preserved.

The pottery designs designate rain, fruition symbols, birds, and flowers, which are arranged with little rhythmic repetition, being scattered over the surface. The pottery, which was formerly black-on-white, now shows some red in the decoration.

PLATE 33

Plate 34

Reference:
Illustrated Catalogue of the Collection Obtained from
the Indians of New Mexico and Arizona in 1879.
James Stevenson,
Second Annual Report Bureau of Ethnology, 1883, pp.
307-465.

a Fig. 514, No. 41609
b Fig. 531, No. 41391
c Fig. 518, No. 41363
d Fig. 518, No. 41363
e Fig. 532, No. 41390
f Fig. 519, No. 41366
g Fig. 514, No. 41609
h Fig. 514, No. 41609

The pueblo of Walpi is situated on the First Mesa of Hopiland in Arizona, on
one side of which are three rows of terraced houses, and on the other a precipice. A
snake dance, the culmination of a nine-day ceremony for rain, is performed in mid-
summer of every alternate year.

The Hopi of Walpi have developed an exceptionally beautiful type of pottery,
of which there are all too few examples extant. They produced a white decorated ware
similar to that of the Zuñi, using triangular figures, curved line designs and birds.

Commencing about the year 1895, Nampeyo, a woman of the pueblo of Hano, has
practically revolutionized the decoration of Hopi pottery by introducing adaptations
of the designs on prehistoric Hopi earthenware.

PLATE 34

a

b

c

d

e

f

g

h

Plate 35

MODERN HOPI, ARIZONA. PUEBLO GROUP
POTTERY DESIGNS

References:
Pueblo Pottery Making
Carl E. Guthe
The Rain-makers
Mary R. Coolidge
The Pueblo Potter
Ruth Bunzel

a   Page 119, No. 14, appendix 2, plate XXXIV, Ruth Bunzel
b   Page 118, No. 1, appendix 2, plate XXXIII, Ruth Bunzel
c   Page 118, No. 5, appendix 2, plate XXXIII, Ruth Bunzel
d   Page 118, No. 2, appendix 2, plate XXXIII, Ruth Bunzel
e   Page 119, No. 15, appendix 2, plate XXXIV, Ruth Bunzel

The period of modern Hopi design goes back to about 1850, that is, the period of intimate contact with civilization. The artists are entirely unconscious of the principles of design in their work, and with no guide except perception of form, they produce an accurately finished vessel. A young girl, when given instruction, is told, "Paint anything you like, only put it on straight." The potter is not influenced by the meaning of her design, except in the use of symbols on pottery designed for ceremonial use. Originality and individuality are general with all potters, and she paints to please herself only, although she may be influenced by the prevailing fashion.

PLATE 35

Plate 36

Modern Hopi, Arizona. Pueblo Group Pottery Designs

References:
> Pueblo Pottery Making
> Carl E. Guthe
> The Rain-makers
> Mary R. Coolidge
> The Pueblo Potter
> Ruth Bunzel

a   Page 119, No. 17, appendix 2, plate XXXIV, Ruth Bunzel
b   Page 118, No. 3, appendix 2, plate XXXIII, Ruth Bunzel
c   Page 118, No. 1, appendix 2, plate XXXIII, Ruth Bunzel
d   Page 119, No. 18, appendix 2, plate XXXIV, Ruth Bunzel
e   Page 39 b, plate XV, Ruth Bunzel

The present mode of Hopi pottery is a renewal of the ancient type illustrated by Sikyatki ware. In the jars of this modern ware the decoration is principally on the upper part, but extends over the surface to just below the shoulder. The design is bordered at the inner edge by a broad black band, with a similar band at the outer edge. Within a few years this new style has completely displaced the old types of ware, due to a love for the ancient and more pleasing symbolic patterns adapted by Nampeyo, as before mentioned.

PLATE 36

a

b

c

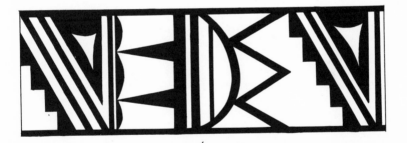

d

e

Plate 37

Reference:

The Zuñi Indians: their Mythology, Esoteric Fraternities, and Ceremonies.
Matilda Coxe Stevenson,
Twenty-third Annual Report Bureau of American Ethnology, 1904, pp. 3-608.

a Plate LIV, Mask of Sáyatäsha
b Plate LXXIV, Mask of Hémishikwe
c Plate LXX, Mask of Úwanami
d Plate LVa, Mask of Yámuhakto
e Plate XLIIIb, Mask of Shíwani

The Zuñi have preserved their strong individuality by extreme exclusiveness, and by so doing may claim their high position. They have developed a philosophy which has been profoundly influenced by their environment and upon which is built a highly complicated ceremonial system which has as its object the tribal welfare and success in all undertakings. Their sacred personages, of whom there are very many, are represented in ceremony by performers who wear decorated masks and are elaborately costumed. The masks are usually of leather highly ornamented with symbolic devices.

PLATE 37

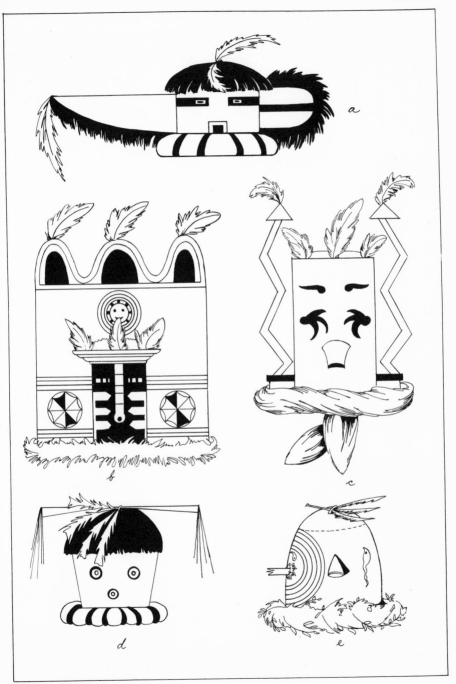

a

b

c

d

e

Plate 38

References:
Yuman Tribes of the Gila River
    Leslie Spier
The North American Indian, vol. II, 1908, pp. 81-88.
Southwest Museum.

a   Page 109, plate VIIh, Leslie Spier
b   Southwest Museum
c   Southwest Museum
d   Page 317, fig. 13a, Leslie Spier
e   Page 109, Fig. 7c, Leslie Spier
f   Page 109, plate VIIf, Leslie Spier
g   Page 109, fig. 7e, Leslie Spier

The Maricopa, a small tribe of the Yuman family, reside in southern Arizona not far from Phoenix. They have developed an interesting type of basketry and pottery designs, but borrowed their method of weaving from the Pimas. For their basketry it was customary to use the tisal willow, squaw-weed, root of the tule, and martynia, or devil's claw; leaves of the yucca being used as a filler for the inner coil. The one tool that is always used in basket making is a bone awl, which at death is buried with the artisan.

The designs are striking and varied, the fret being used in combination with circular forms of the swastika. As their artistic faculty developed, practice brought increased skill, and some examples of their baskets, pottery, and weaving are exquisitely beautiful.

PLATE 38

a

b

c

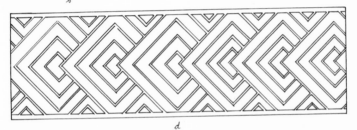

d

e

f

g

Plate 39

References:

Aboriginal American Basketry: Studies in a Textile Art
without Machinery.
Otis Tufton Mason,
Annual Report of the U. S. National Museum for 1902,
pp. 171-548.
Indian Basketry,
George Wharton James

a Southwest Museum, pottery design
b Southwest Museum, beadwork
c Southwest Museum, beadwork
d Southwest Museum, beadwork
e Southwest Museum, beadwork

The Mohave, who gave name to that vast arid waste, the Mohave Desert, are of Yuman stock, like the Maricopas, who have lived for centuries in the valley of the Rio Colorado in California and Arizona. In early times the Mohave were a powerful tribe, but owing to outside influences they have become greatly diminished in number.

The beadwork made by the women is interesting in design; the patterns are made up of so-called symbols combined in various ways. The meaning of these designs is not fixed, so the same symbols are often given different meanings even by persons within the tribe. The Indian artists picture in their work the common objects of everyday life; the great powers of nature, the sun, moon, stars, wind, trees, animals, birds, or whatever might suit their fancy. On clothing, designs were sometimes used that were supposed to have power to protect the wearer from harm. Many of the designs are worked on a white background representing the snow-time, or winter, which was the season when the men went on the war trail to achieve honors and glory. Other colors symbolic of military achievement were red, indicating wounds inflicted or received; yellow the sun-colored war horses, and green, representing the grass or summer. In religious or ceremonial designs, red represents the sunset or thunder; blue, the sky, water or day; yellow, the dawn or sunlight; and black, the night.

PLATE 39

a

b

c

d

e

Plate 40

References:
Basketry of the San Carlos Apache
Helen H. Roberts,
Anthropological Papers of the American Museum of
Natural History, 1929, vol. XXXI, pt. 3.
Illustrated History of Baskets and Plates, made by California Indians and many other tribes.
T. A. Roseberry collection

a   Page 198, fig. 27, Helen H. Roberts
b   Page 198, fig. 27, Helen H. Roberts
c   Page 183, fig. 22b, Helen H. Roberts
d   Page 178, fig. 19g, Helen H. Roberts
e   Plate 18, T. A. Roseberry collection

A small band of people numbering 1172, the San Carlos Apache, live along the main stream and nearer branches of the Gila River to the east of Phoenix, Arizona.

The San Carlos Apache do not use grass in their baskets, but only the shoots of shrubs and young trees, which accounts for the rigidity of their product. Occasionally modern baskets display a touch of red in the color scheme of black and cream, with delightful effect. The material which furnishes the red is the root of the yucca.

These people make three distinct types of baskets: water-jars, carrying baskets, and food bowls of every kind. The bowls are for holding meal, winnowing grain, parching corn, boiling food, mashing berries, mixing dough, and laundry purposes; in fact a bowl or tray is needed by the Indian woman in much the same way as by her white sister. Their twined basketry is crude in texture in design, and in the colors used for the designs. On the other hand, their coiled baskets show the handiwork of an art-loving people. The designs are checkerwork, zigzag, triangles, and diamonds with diagonal, vertical, or horizontal lines. The introduction of human or animal figures, sometimes grotesque, is of comparatively recent origin. The square and rectangle are entirely absent as separate figures, occuring only in some sort of checker formation. Triangles and diamonds are worked in solid colors, usually black, since the background is cream. The adaptation of the size of design to the form of the background field illustrates clearly that the San Carlos artistic sense is of an unusually high order.

PLATE 40

Plate 41

White Mountain, Arizona and Mescalero Apache, New Mexico
Basket and Dress Ornament

References:

A Study of the Textile Art in its Relation to the Development of Form and Color.
William H. Holmes,
Sixth Annual Report Bureau of Ethnology, 1888, pp. 189-252.
Annual Report of the Smithsonian Institution, 1928.
Specimens from Southwest Museum.
Indian Basketry,
George Wharton James

a   Southwest Museum
b   Southwest Museum
c   Plate 17, Report Smithsonian Institution, 1928
d   Page 223, fig. 325, William H. Holmes
e   Southwest Museum
f   Southwest Museum

The Apache are to be found in New Mexico and Arizona. A warlike nomadic people, the terror of the early white settlers of the Southwest, yet when intelligently treated, no more appreciative or tractable Indians are to be found.

The Apache are expert basket-makers, proud of the fineness of their work, extremely poetic in the designs they conceive, and artistic in their arrangement. The designs usually consist of small figures with a sense of ease approaching realism.

PLATE 41

Plate 42

PAPAGO, ARIZONA-SONORA
POTTERY DESIGNS

References:
Basketry of the Papago and Pima,
Mary L. Kissell,
Anthropological Papers of the American Museum of
Natural History, 1916, vol. XVII, pp. 115-264.

a   Page 213, fig. 59e
b   Page 213, fig. 59f
c   Page 218, fig. 64b
d   Page 219, fig. 65c
e   Page 239, fig. 77
f   Page 240, fig. 78

The Papago live in southern Arizona and northwestern Sonora. Possibly in no other spot in North America has the Indian been less influenced by white men, so that old customs persist, even to the tattooing of the face by older men and women.

Like all desert regions, plant growth was hindered in its struggle for existence, and the desert vegetation exerted an influence upon the activities of the tribes, and the tribes in turn have adapted themselves to the limitations of the desert, hence much effort and skill were required to discover the materials most suitable for basket-making. Excellent coiled baskets have been produced by Papago women, but it is said that many of them have been sacrificed by burning on the death of the owners.

PLATE 42

Plate 43

PAPAGO, ARIZONA-SONORA
POTTERY DESIGNS

References:
Basketry of the Papago and Pima,
Mary L. Kissell,
Anthropological Papers of the American Museum of
Natural History, 1916, vol. XVII, pp. 115-264.

a   Page 221, fig. 67d
b   Page 223, fig. 69
c   Page 221, fig. 67c
d   Page 213, fig. 59b
e   Page 239, fig. 77
f   Page 216, fig. 62c

Distinctive differences between the basketry designs of the Pima and the Papago are found. The influence of the environment is felt, since the supply of martynia gives Papago a dominance of dark over light in their baskets. Aside from the dissimilarity in dark and light, the bands differ obviously in shape, proportion, and general contour. One is impressed by the strong feeling for large masses of dark and light in comparison to the feeling for line of the Pima. The Papago woman deals mostly with a horizontal line in her work, which gives a restful quality to the design. They have a distinct number of typical designs, namely, the encircling fret, the horizontal band arranged in a variety of ways, and the vertical fret.

Papago design is dignified and reserved, handled in a simple, strong, and direct manner.

PLATE 43

Plate 44

PIMA, ARIZONA
BASKET AND POTTERY DESIGNS

Reference:
The Pima Indians
Frank Russell,
Twenty-sixth Annual Report Bureau of American Eth-

nology, 1908, pp. 3-389.
a Plate XXVII, d
b Plate XXVIII, a
c Plate XXV, a
d Plate XXVII, e
e Plate XVIII, c
f Plate XIX, f

The Pima inhabit a reservation in southern Arizona not far from Phoenix, and have always been noted for their quiet and peaceful character. They have developed a high type of basketry which contains some intricate patterns that resemble Greek and Oriental figures; in the variations of the swastika alone they show splendid examples. Many of their designs represent the source of water supply in the center, with radiating geometric lines representing the winding streams.

In the construction of their baskets the Pima use the tisal willow, squaw weed, skunk weed, the root of the tule, and martyina, or devil's claw.

PLATE 44

a

b

c

d

e

f

Plate 45

PIMA, ARIZONA
BASKETRY DESIGNS

Reference:
The Pima Indians
Frank Russell,
Twenty-sixth Annual Report Bureau of American Ethnology, 1908, pp 3, 390.

a   Plate XXXII, c
b   Plate XXX, h
c   Plate XXIX, c
d   Plate XX, e
e   Plate XXXI, f
f   Page 130, fig. 55

    In Pima basketry there is a dominance of light over dark color, with a feeling for line which is expressed in a network of black. Horizontal lines are used in a secondary way, being held in subservience to a more dominant motif, the spiral and whorl. The patterns are the fret, rectangular whorl, triangular whorl, spiral rosette, and terrace. The fret is the oldest and most common design. The whorl consists of four central twirling rectangular arms with a repeating whorl at the rim. Obliques are frequently composed of a line of small triangles forming a terraced design.

    Pima work is replete with action and grace; it is elaborate, delicate, and intricate; the technique is clear-cut and perfect in craftsmanship.

PLATE 45

a

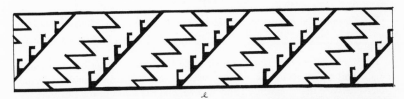

b

c

d

e

f

Plate 46

CHEMEHUEVI, ARIZONA-CALIFORNIA
BASKET DESIGNS

References:

Aboriginal American Basketry: Studies in a Textile Art
without Machinery.
Otis Tufton Mason,
Annual Report of the U. S. National Museum for 1902,
pp. 171-548.
Basketry of the San Carlos Apache
Helen H. Roberts,
Anthropological Papers of the American Museum of
Natural History, 1929, vol. XXXI, pt. 3.

a   Plate 231, vol. 2, Otis Tufton Mason
b   Plate 231, vol. 2, Otis Tufton Mason
c   Page 180, fig. 21, Helen H. Roberts
d   Page 179, fig. 20, Helen H. Roberts
e   Plate 231, Otis Tufton Mason
f   Plate 231, Otis Tufton Mason

The Chemehuevi live along the Colorado river north of the Mohave. They produce basketry similar to that of the San Carlos Apache, hence there is a tendency to
confuse the two.

Horizontal arrangements are typical, while radiating or whorling distributions
are rare. This difference in design arrangement is one of the distinguishing features
of the basketry of the Chemehuevi and Apache, also the finish of the rim coil; were
it not for this it would be difficult to discriminate the products of the two tribes. Hence
it is more by feel, which comes only with study, than by rule that the basket lover
may learn to recognize the work of the various Indians.

PLATE 46

a

b

c

d

e

f

Plate 47

References:
> The Navaho and his Blanket
> U. S. Hollister
> Navaho Weaving
> Charles Avery Amsden
> Design detail from blankets, Southwest Museum
> Design detail from blankets, Mrs. Kenneth Worthen
> Design detail from blankets, Mrs. F. R. Smith

a   Mrs. Kenneth Worthen
b   Southwest Museum
c   Mrs. Kenneth Worthen
d   Southwest Museum
e   Southwest Museum
f   Mrs. F. R. Smith
g   Mrs. F. R. Smith
h   Mrs. Kenneth Worthen
i   Southwest Museum
j   Mrs. F. R. Smith

The Navaho are a semi-nomadic Athapascan tribe occupying a reservation in northern Arizona, northwest New Mexico, and southern Utah. Numbering about 40,000, they are the most populous tribe in the United States.

They are a picturesque people whose principal interests are blanket weaving, sheep herding, and the manufacture of silver and turquoise jewelry. The Navaho shear their sheep, wash, dye, card, spin, and weave the wool into attractive and valuable blankets. The primitive art of weaving is many centuries old, but so far as known the Navaho acquired the art from captive Pueblo women not earlier than the latter part of the eighteenth century.

PLATE 47

Plate 48

NAVAHO, ARIZONA-NEW MEXICO. NOMADIC GROUP
PATTERNS AND FIGURES FROM DRY PAINTINGS OF DSÍLYIDJE-QÁCAL.

Reference:
The Mountain Chant.
Washington Matthews,
Fifth Annual Report Bureau of Ethnology, 1887, pp. 379-467.

a Plate XVI
b Plate XVI
c Plate XV
d Plate XV
e Plate XVI
f Plate XVI

Sand to the depth of two inches is spread on the floor, then smoothed and evened with a curved stick; on this sand the artist works from the center outward with colors made by a man sitting at the east. Yellow, red, and white are made by grinding native rocks; black is made from charcoal. Black and white are mixed to produce a gray-blue.

The four sacred colors of the cardinal points are, white for the East, blue for the West, yellow for the South, and black for the North.

The artist then takes a pinch of the desired color between his thumb and forefinger and lets it trickle in the line of his proposed design, when the pattern is finished, with its exquisite color and detail, a rare work of art is produced.

PLATE 48

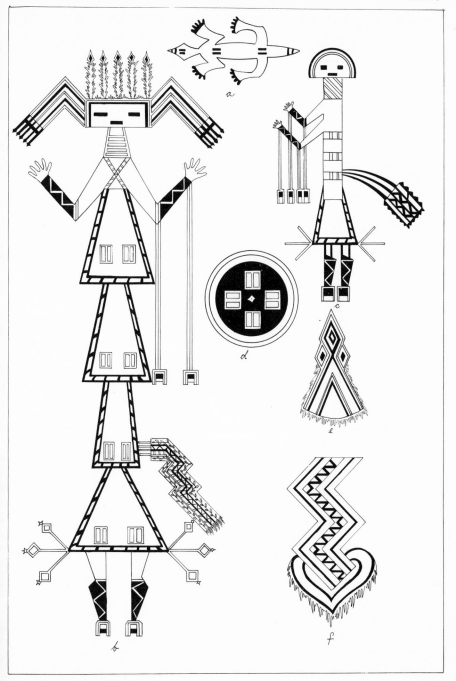

Plate 49

NAVAHO, ARIZONA-NEW MEXICO. NOMADIC GROUP
PATTERNS AND FIGURES FROM DRY PAINTINGS OF DŚILYIDJE-QÁCAL.

Reference:
The Mountain Chant.
Fifth Annual Report Bureau of Ethnology, 1887, pp.
379-467.

a   Plate XVII
b   Plate XVII
c   Plate XVII
d   Plate XVII
e   Plate XVII
f   Plate XVII
g   Plate XVII
h   Plate XVII
i   Plate XVIII

Every ceremony has its own dry painting, and these represent a very old traditional art which was borrowed from the Pueblos. The essence of Navaho art is an
arrangement and repetition of a few elements, either in stripes or around a central
motif, or spotting against a plain or striped background. The keynote of their work is a
large mass of perfect simplicity, and continuous repetition of quiet inert design.

PLATE 49

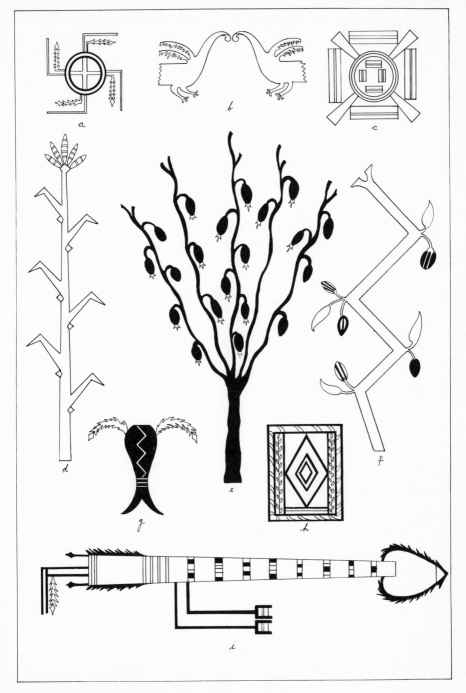

Plate 50

NAVAHO, ARIZONA-NEW MEXICO. NOMADIC GROUP
ANCIENT AND MODERN RUG DESIGNS

References:
Navaho Weavers and their Work.
Washington Matthews,
Third Annual Report Bureau of Ethnology, 1884, pp.
371-391.
Design detail from blankets, Southwest Museum.
Design detail from blanket, collection of Mrs. Kenneth
Worthen.

a   Southwest Museum
b   Southwest Museum
c   Southwest Museum
d   Mrs. Kenneth Worthen
e   Southwest Museum
f   Southwest Museum

The women who have controlled the weaving industry for two centuries originally had only three natural colors to use, a rusty black, white, and a brownish gray; herbs and a desert brush were used to produce livlier shades. To intensify the black a dye was made of sumac, ochre, and piñon boiled together. Similarly was invented a dark blue, several shades of yellow, and a reddish color.

The women who for generations have been weaving from their imagination follow no visible pattern, yet the design, color, and proportion in the hands of an experienced weaver come out nearly perfect.

PLATE 50

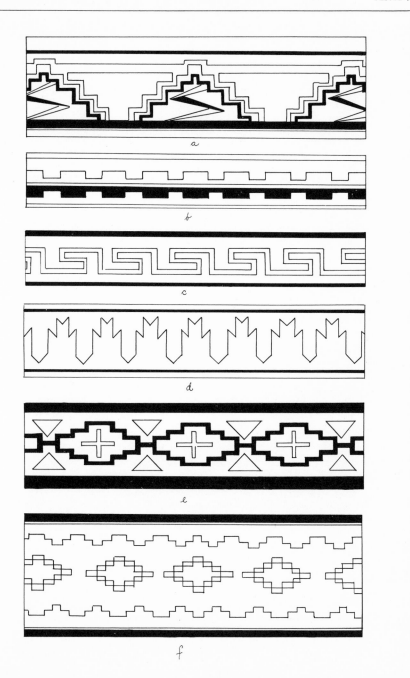

a

b

c

d

e

f

Dover Books on Art

Dover Books on Art

LANDSCAPE GARDENING IN JAPAN, Josiah Conder. A detailed picture of Japanese gardening techniques and ideas, the artistic principles incorporated in the Japanese garden, and the religious and ethical concepts at the heart of those principles. Preface. 92 illustrations, plus all 40 full-page plates from the Supplement. Index. xv + 299pp. 8⅜ x 11¼.

T1216 Paperbound $2.75

DESIGN AND FIGURE CARVING, E. J. Tangerman. "Anyone who can peel a potato can carve," states the author, and in this unusual book he shows you how, covering every stage in detail from very simple exercises working up to museum-quality pieces. Terrific aid for hobbyists, arts and crafts counselors, teachers, those who wish to make reproductions for the commercial market. Appendix: How to Enlarge a Design. Brief bibliography. Index. 1298 figures. x + 289pp. 5⅜ x 8½.

T1209 Paperbound $1.85

WILD FOWL DECOYS, Joel Barber. Antique dealers, collectors, craftsmen, hunters, readers of Americana, etc. will find this the only thorough and reliable guide on the market today to this unique folk art. It contains the history, cultural significance, regional design variations; unusual decoy lore; working plans for constructing decoys; and loads of illustrations. 140 full-page plates, 4 in color. 14 additional plates of drawings and plans by the author. xxvii + 156pp. 7⅞ x 10¾.   T11 Paperbound $2.75

1800 WOODCUTS BY THOMAS BEWICK AND HIS SCHOOL. This is the largest collection of first-rate pictorial woodcuts in print—an indispensable part of the working library of every commercial artist, art director, production designer, packaging artist, craftsman, manufacturer, librarian, art collector, and artist. And best of all, when you buy your copy of Bewick, you buy the rights to reproduce individual illustrations—no permission needed, no acknowledgments, no clearance fees! Classified index. Bibliography and sources. xiv + 246pp. 9 x 12.

T766 Clothbound $10.00

THE SCRIPT LETTER, Tommy Thompson. Prepared by a noted authority, this is a thorough, straightforward course of instruction with advice on virtually every facet of the art of script lettering. Also a brief history of lettering with examples from early copy books and illustrations from present day advertising and packaging. Copiously illustrated. Bibliography. 128pp. 6½ x 9⅛.   T1311 Paperbound $1.00

Dover Books on Art

GREEK REVIVAL ARCHITECTURE IN AMERICA, T. Hamlin. A comprehensive study of the American Classical Revival, its regional variations, reasons for its success and eventual decline. Profusely illustrated with photos, sketches, floor plans and sections, displaying the work of almost every important architect of the time. 2 appendices. 39 figures, 94 plates containing 221 photos, 62 architectural designs, drawings, etc. 324-item classified bibliography. Index. xi + 439pp. 5⅜ x 8½.

T1148 Paperbound $3.00

CREATIVE LITHOGRAPHY AND HOW TO DO IT, Grant Arnold. Written by a man who practiced and taught lithography for many years, this highly useful volume explains all the steps of the lithographic process from tracing the drawings on the stone to printing the lithograph, with helpful hints for solving special problems. Index. 16 reproductions of lithographs. 11 drawings. xv + 214pp. of text. 5⅜ x 8½.

T1208 Paperbound $1.65

TEACH YOURSELF ANTIQUE COLLECTING, E. Bradford. An excellent, brief guide to collecting British furniture, silver, pictures and prints, pewter, pottery and porcelain, Victoriana, enamels, clocks or other antiques. Much background information difficult to find elsewhere. 15pp. of illus. 215pp. 7 x 4¼.

Clothbound $2.00

THE STANDARD BOOK OF QUILT MAKING AND COLLECTING, M. Ickis. Even if you are a beginner, you will soon find yourself quilting like an expert, by following these clearly drawn patterns, photographs, and step-by-step instructions. Learn how to plan the quilt, to select the pattern to harmonize with the design and color of the room, to choose materials. Over 40 full-size patterns. Index. 483 illustrations. One color plate. xi + 276pp. 6¾ x 9½.

T582 Paperbound $2.00

THE ENJOYMENT AND USE OF COLOR, W. Sargent. Requiring no special technical know-how, this book tells you all about color and how it is created, perceived, and imitated in art. Covers many little-known facts about color values, intensities, effects of high and low illumination, complementary colors, and color harmonies. Simple do-it-yourself experiments and observations. 35 illustrations, including 6 full-page color plates. New color frontispiece. Index. x + 274 pp. 5⅜ x 8.

T944 Paperbound $2.00

Dover Books on Art

DECORATIVE ART OF THE SOUTHWESTERN INDIANS,
D. S. Sides. 300 black and white reproductions from one of the most beautiful art traditions of the primitive world, ranging from the geometric art of the Great Pueblo period of the 13th century to modern folk art. Motives from basketry, beadwork, Zuni masks, Hopi kachina dolls, Navajo sand pictures and blankets, and ceramic ware. Unusual and imaginative designs will inspire craftsmen in all media, and commercial artists may reproduce any of them without permission or payment. xviii + 101pp. 5⅝ x 8⅜.   T139 Paperbound $1.00

PENNSYLVANIA DUTCH AMERICAN FOLK ART, H. J. Kauffman. The originality and charm of this early folk art give it a special appeal even today, and surviving pieces are sought by collectors all over the country. Here is a rewarding introductory guide to the Dutch country and its household art, concentrating on pictorial matter—hex signs, tulip ware, weather vanes, interiors, paintings and folk sculpture, rocking horses and children's toys, utensils, Stiegel-type glassware, etc. "A serious, worthy and helpful volume," W. G. Dooley, N. Y. TIMES. Introduction. Bibliography. 279 halftone illustrations. 28 motifs and other line drawings. 1 map. 146pp. 7⅞ x 10¾.
T1205 Paperbound $2.00

DESIGN AND EXPRESSION IN THE VISUAL ARTS, J. F. A. Taylor. Here is a much needed discussion of art theory which relates the new and sometimes bewildering directions of 20th century art to the great traditions of the past. The first discussion of principle that addresses itself to the eye rather than to the intellect, using illustrations from Rembrandt, Leonardo, Mondrian, El Greco, etc. List of plates. Index. 59 reproductions. 5 color plates. 75 figures. x + 245pp. 5⅜ x 8½.
T1195 Paperbound $1.75

GRAPHIC REPRODUCTION IN PRINTING, H. Curwen. A behind-the-scenes account of the various processes of graphic reproduction—relief, intaglio, stenciling, lithography, line methods, continuous tone methods, photogravure, collotype—and the advantages and limitations of each. Invaluable for all artists, advertising art directors, commercial designers, advertisers, publishers, and all art lovers who buy prints as a hobby. 137 illustrations, including 13 full-page plates, 10 in color. xvi + 171pp. 5¼ x 8½.   T512 Clothbound $6.00

Dover Books on Art

A HANDBOOK OF ANATOMY FOR ART STUDENTS, Arthur Thomson. This long-popular text teaches any student, regardless of level of technical competence, all the subtleties of human anatomy. Clear photographs, numerous line sketches and diagrams of bones, joints, etc. Use it as a text for home study, as a supplement to life class work, or as a lifelong sourcebook and reference volume. Author's prefaces. 67 plates, containing 40 line drawings, 86 photographs—mostly full page. 211 figures. Appendix. Index. xx + 459pp. 5⅜ x 8⅜.   T1163 Paperbound $3.00

WHITTLING AND WOODCARVING, E. J. Tangerman. With this book, a beginner who is moderately handy can whittle or carve scores of useful objects, toys for children, gifts, or simply pass hours creatively and enjoyably. "Easy as well as instructive reading," N. Y. Herald Tribune Books. 464 illustrations, with appendix and index. x + 293pp. 5½ x 8⅛.
                                        T965 Paperbound $1.75

ONE HUNDRED AND ONE PATCHWORK PATTERNS, Ruby Short McKim. Whether you have made a hundred quilts or none at all, you will find this the single most useful book on quilt-making. There are 101 full patterns (all exact size) with full instructions for cutting and sewing. In addition there is some really choice folklore about the origin of the ingenious pattern names: "Monkey Wrench," "Road to California," "Drunkard's Path," "Crossed Canoes," to name a few. Over 500 illustrations. 124 pp. 7⅞ x 10¾.   T773 Paperbound $1.85

ART AND GEOMETRY, W. M. Ivins, Jr. Challenges the idea that the foundations of modern thought were laid in ancient Greece. Pitting Greek tactile-muscular intuitions of space against modern visual intuitions, the author, for 30 years curator of prints, Metropolitan Museum of Art, analyzes the differences between ancient and Renaissance painting and sculpture and tells of the first fruitful investigations of perspective. x + 113pp. 5⅜ x 8⅜.   T941 Paperbound $1.00

TEACH YOURSELF TO STUDY SCULPTURE, Wm. Gaunt. Useful details on the sculptor's art and craft, tools, carving and modeling; its relation to other arts; ways to look at sculpture; sculpture of the East and West; etc. "Useful both to the student and layman and a good refresher for the professional sculptor," Prof. J. Skeaping, Royal College of Art. 32 plates, 24 figures. Index. xii + 155pp. 7 x 4¼.   Clothbound $2.00

Dover Books on Art

STYLES IN PAINTING, Paul Zucker. By comparing paintings of similar subject matter, the author shows the characteristics of various painting styles. You are shown at a glance the differences between reclining nudes by Giorgione, Velasquez, Goya, Modigliani; how a Byzantine portrait. is unlike a portrait by Van Eyck, da Vinci, Dürer, or Marc Chagall; how the painting of landscapes has changed gradually from ancient Pompeii to Lyonel Feininger in our own century. 241 beautiful, sharp photographs illustrate the text. xiv + 338 pp. 5⅝ x 8¼.

T760 Paperbound $2.00

THE PRACTICE OF TEMPERA PAINTING, D. V. Thompson, Jr. Used in Egyptian and Minoan wall paintings and in much of the fine work of Giotto, Botticelli, Titian, and many others, tempera has long been regarded as one of the finest painting methods known. This is the definitive work on the subject by the world's outstanding authority. He covers the uses and limitations of tempera, designing, drawing with the brush, incising outlines, applying to metal, mixing and preserving tempera, varnishing and guilding, etc. Appendix, "Tempera Practice in Yale Art School" by Prof. L. E. York. 4 full page plates. 85 illustrations. x + 141pp. 5⅜ x 8½.

T343 Paperbound $1.50

GRAPHIC WORLDS OF PETER BRUEGEL THE ELDER, H. A. Klein. 64 of the finest etchings and engravings made from the drawings of the Flemish master Peter Bruegel. Every aspect of the artist's diversified style and subject matter is represented, with notes providing biographical and other background information. Excellent reproductions on opaque stock with nothing on reverse side. 63 engravings, 1 woodcut. Bibliography. xviii + 289pp. 11⅜ x 8¼.

T1132 Paperbound $3.00

A HISTORY OF ENGRAVING AND ETCHING, A. M. Hind. Beginning with the anonymous masters of 15th century engraving, this highly regarded and thorough survey carries you through Italy, Holland, and Germany to the great engravers and beginnings of etching in the 16th century, through the portrait engravers, master etchers, practicioners of mezzotint, crayon manner and stipple, aquatint, color prints, to modern etching in the period just prior to World War I. Beautifully illustrated —sharp clear prints on heavy opaque paper. Author's preface. 3 appendixes. 111 illustrations. xviii + 487 pp. 5⅜ x 8½.

T954 Paperbound $2.75

THE COMPLETE BOOK OF SILK SCREEN PRINTING PRO-DUCTION, J. I. Biegeleisen. Here is a clear and complete picture of every aspect of silk screen technique and press operation—from individually operated manual presses to modern automatic ones. Unsurpassed as a guidebook for setting up shop, making shop operation more efficient, finding out about latest methods and equipment; or as a textbook for use in teaching, studying, or learning all aspects of the profession. 124 figures. Index. Bibliography. List of Supply Sources. xi + 253pp. $5\frac{3}{8}$ x $8\frac{1}{2}$.

T1100 Paperbound $2.00

A HISTORY OF COSTUME, Carl Köhler. The most reliable and authentic account of the development of dress from ancient times through the 19th century. Based on actual pieces of clothing that have survived, using paintings, statues and other reproductions only where originals no longer exist. Hundreds of illustrations, including detailed patterns for many articles. Highly useful for theatre and movie directors, fashion designers, illustrators, teachers. Edited and augmented by Emma von Sichart. Translated by Alexander K. Dallas. 594 illustrations. 464pp. $5\frac{1}{8}$ x $7\frac{1}{8}$.

T1030 Paperbound $2.75

CHINESE HOUSEHOLD FURNITURE, G. N. Kates. A summary of virtually everything that is known about authentic Chinese furniture before it was contaminated by the influence of the West. The text covers history of styles, materials used, principles of design and craftsmanship, and furniture arrangement—all fully illustrated. xiii + 190pp. $5\frac{5}{8}$ x $8\frac{1}{2}$.

T958 Paperbound $1.50

THE COMPLETE WOODCUTS OF ALBRECHT DÜRER, edited by Dr. Willi Kurth. Albrecht Dürer was a master in various media, but it was in woodcut design that his creative genius reached its highest expression. Here are all of his extant woodcuts, a collection of over 300 great works, many of which are not available elsewhere. An indispensable work for the art historian and critic and all art lovers. 346 plates. Index. 285pp. $8\frac{1}{2}$ x $12\frac{1}{4}$.

T1097 Paperbound $2.50

Dover publishes books on commercial art, art history, crafts, design, art classics; also books on music, literature, science, mathematics, puzzles and entertainments, chess, engineering, biology, philosophy, psychology, languages, history, and other fields. For free circulars write to Dept. DA, Dover Publications, Inc., 180 Varick St., New York, N.Y. 10014.